For information visit:

http://www.funbooksforyou.com

ISBN-10: 1544802080
ISBN-13 : 978-1544802084

First Edition: March 2017

10  9  8  7  6  5  4  3  2  1

She purrs when you touch her
in the right spot.
Rub her here and she'll blow her top.

My pussy likes to play with the
big black cock.
She can keep up with the
biggest of jogs.

She'll shake, purr, and love you forever.
Just give her attention, and forget her never.

Her purrs sound smooth as silk.
She'll especially go wild if you
give her some milk.

You can play with my pussy in the great outdoors.

When you're tired, you can go inside and play with her around the floors.

But she's a jealous pussy, and she'll surely hiss, if you play with other pussies.
She knows something's amiss!

Sometimes my pussy sheds.
It goes everywhere!
If only my pussy didn't have
so much hair.

That's why I must brush my pussy day and night.
Keep her nice and clean until I find the man that is right.

She loves to play, and does as she please.
She especially loves it when you tease.

I spend hours keeping my pussy clean as that's my wish.
I don't want my pussy to smell like fish

My pussy is always hungry, always eating from her bowl.
Keeping her full is a huge toll.

She's not picky; everything you put near her mouth, she'll eat.
But she especially likes her meat.

My pussy will keep playing and won't stop.
She's truly someone you should adopt.

If you don't want to play with my pussy, I have something else to make you last.
Come to the barn and play with my ass.

For more fun books like this, visit:
www.FunBooksForYou.com

Made in the USA
Las Vegas, NV
16 November 2023